Original title:
Coral Dreams

Copyright © 2025 Creative Arts Management OÜ
All rights reserved.

Author: Juliette Kensington
ISBN HARDBACK: 978-1-80587-346-4
ISBN PAPERBACK: 978-1-80587-816-2

The Depths Where Dreams Swim

In a realm where fish wear hats,
And jellyfish dance in polka spots.
An octopus plays the accordion,
While sea cucumbers plot big shots.

Clams gossip about lonely snails,
Starfish spinning silly tales.
With a wink, a whale sings a tune,
And crabs do the cha-cha in seashell trails.

Intricate Brushstrokes of Nature

In this canvas, fish paint the day,
With bubble art that floats away.
Anemones tickle the clownish crew,
As sea horses strut in dance they view.

Watercolor waves crash with glee,
While turtles joke about their speed.
With a flick of fins, the fun's begun,
In this gallery, we laugh and run.

Twilight of the Tides

As tides recede, the silliness swells,
Where seaweed waves its wavy spells.
Clownfish giggle, and dolphins leap,
Making splashes that twirl and sweep.

The moon winks down, a playful sight,
While shrimp throw a disco ball night.
In this twilight, laughter galore,
As fishy friends dance on the shore.

The Ocean's Secret Symphony

A symphony plays under the surf,
With whales conducting, what a turf!
Bubble notes rise and drift on by,
As squids ink charts to the sky.

Clown antics steal the show with flair,
While crabs build castles without a care.
Each wave a chord in this ocean song,
Where goofy rhythms keep us strong.

Shimmering Depths

In the sea where fish wear hats,
Octopuses dance with sassy cats.
Bubbles giggle, tickling toes,
While starfish play the castaway shows.

Waves at play, like kids at school,
Smiling shells are no one's fool.
A crab rolls by, quite dressed to impress,
His claw clinks like a playful press.

Liquid Lullabies

Seahorses hum a sleepy tune,
While jellyfish float, a lighted balloon.
A fish with a mustache sings out loud,
Charming the crowd, oh so proud!

Mermaids tossing seafood in jest,
With clams that giggle, they're not like the rest.
Kelp sways gently, a dance of delight,
As the moon winks goodnight.

Fragments of an Ocean's Heart

Turtles tell tales of old sunken gold,
While shrimps strike poses, oh so bold.
A dolphin slides in, full of flair,
Chatting with crabs in a playful air.

Seashells giggle, with secrets to share,
Winking at waves with a salty glare.
The ocean's pulse, sweet and bright,
Keeps everyone laughing deep into the night.

Enchanted Fathoms

In deep waters where laughter is found,
Eels do a shimmy, spinning around.
Fish in pajamas throw confetti with glee,
While sea cucumbers sip on tea.

A whale rolls by, his jokes are a blast,
Making bubbles that shimmer and last.
With flip-flops made of seaweed so fine,
The ocean's a party, and everyone shines.

Oceanic Reverie

Bubbles rise with giggles, fresh,
Fish wear hats that look quite posh.
Octopus plays on a chess board,
While turtles dance like they're on tour.

Seaweed sways with laughter loud,
Clownfish swimming in a crowd.
Starfish twirl in twenty styles,
As seahorses flash their smiles.

Tidal Whispers

Waves whisper secrets to the sand,
Crabs march proudly, a marching band.
Jellyfish float in silly hats,
While whales giggle at the chitchats.

Seagulls play tag with the breeze,
Chasing their tails like they're at ease.
Dolphins leap to a comical tune,
Underneath the mischief moon.

Vibrant Currents

The clowns of the sea, those tiny fish,
Juggle pearls with a flick and swish.
A sea anemone gives a cheer,
To the goofballs swimming near.

With bubbles popping like balloons,
Starfish groove to underwater tunes.
A playful swell, a twist, a shout,
In this colorful, splashy bout.

Serpent's Flute

A long sea serpent plays a tune,
To the rhythm of waves beneath the moon.
Fish wear sunglasses, shades of blue,
While crabs tap dance; oh what a view!

With each note, the seashells clap,
And dolphins join in with a zap.
An octopus plays the sax with flair,
As the ocean sways in the salty air.

Ages Beneath

In depths where fish wear tiny hats,
The jellyfish dance like silly dancers.
An octopus juggles some rubber mats,
While sea turtles giggle at silly prancers.

The starfish debate over pizza toppings,
A crab sings loud, but he can't hold a tune.
They all dive down, avoiding the plopping,
While the seaweed sways like a big green balloon.

A clownfish tells jokes that make no sense,
But everybody laughs, they have no pretense.
The seahorses queue for the best selfie,
In a world where it's totally never dull and hefty.

So come take a dip in this wacky sea,
Where laughter and bubbles are always free.
Here beneath the waves, let's make some cheer,
With ages of fish that will tickle your ear.

Symphony of Colorful Fins

In waters bright, where fish compose,
A symphony that ever flows.
With fins that flutter, tails that whirl,
An orchestra of colors in a twirl.

The trumpetfish play their silver notes,
While clownfish laugh in tiny boats.
A group of minnows form a choir,
Singing so sweet, they spark our desire.

A grouper joins with an offbeat dance,
While sea horses try their best to prance.
The anemones sway, a perfect stage,
For underwater fun and a wild rage.

So join this concert in the deep blue sea,
Where laughter and tunes meet perfectly.
With every splash, let joyous hearts spin,
In this fun symphony led by fins.

A Siren's Song

Beneath the waves, she sings with glee,
A siren who's lost her buoyancy.
She croons a tune and trips on her hair,
As fish stop by to lend a finful care.

Her voice is loud, but her notes go wrong,
A mix of flounder with a little gong.
The blowfish puff while they giggle and swell,
Telling tales of her song that's a comical spell.

A hero fish ventures to save the day,
With silly antics in a playful ballet.
But ends up tangling in kelp and seaweed,
As the siren sings on, filled with mischief indeed.

So listen well, to her funny refrain,
In the world of the waves, feel the joyous strain.
Where laughter exists beneath the sea's throng,
To the comical twist of a siren's song.

The Enchanted Tangle

Amid the waves, a fish sings loud,
In a tangle of seaweed, wearing a shroud.
Octopus dances, with eight flailing limbs,
Chasing his tail, oh, how he swims.

A crab with a hat, tip-taps on sand,
Claiming the shore, like it's his own land.
Seagulls join in, with their silly squawks,
Belting out songs, while the sea gently rocks.

Strokes of Mesmerizing Light

In underwater galleries, fish paint the sea,
Dancing on currents, as slick as can be.
With strokes of bright colors, they splash and they twirl,
Creating a spectacle, such wonders they whirl.

A jellyfish glows, in a wobbly show,
Modelling fashion, in the moonlight's glow.
Stars look on puzzled, as waves softly giggle,
Amped by the rhythm, they shimmy and wiggle.

Ocean's Poetic Harmony

A whale tells a joke, with a deep, booming voice,
Anemones chuckle, it's hard not to rejoice.
Dolphins race by, with a wink and a grin,
In this watery realm, nobody wears a pin.

Turtles engage in a slow-motion fight,
As octopuses throw confetti of light.
Mackerels swoosh in, leading the parade,
While snails in their shells watch, unbothered and laid.

The Melting Horizon

Where water meets sky, a hue-full affair,
Squids toss confetti, like they just don't care.
Fish in tuxedos, they waddle and sway,
Whispers of silliness fill up the bay.

A sunset adorns the ocean's vast dome,
Reminding the critters, they're never alone.
With giggles and bubbles, the tides laugh and crash,
As waves make a splash, in a colorful flash.

Reflections in the Coral Sand

Underwater daydreams play,
Fish wear glasses, not quite gray.
Starfish dance in disco shoes,
Sea cucumbers sip their brews.

Sharks on surfboards catching rays,
Crabs in shorts, they laugh and stay.
An octopus juggles with glee,
While turtles sing off-key with me.

Bubbles pop like comic strips,
Mermaids join in with silly quips.
Anemones throw a costume bash,
Where sea urchins wave and flash!

In the sun, we twist and sway,
With jellyfish leading the way.
In this undersea parade,
Every quirk is serenade!

Whispers of the Tides

Waves carry secrets with a grin,
Octopi dressed for a night to win.
Seahorses gallop, all a-flutter,
Eating seaweed—oh, what splutter!

Crabs play hopscotch on the shore,
While clams debate what life's for.
Starfish trade their fashion tips,
As dolphins try to flip and slip.

Anemones hide in shy delight,
Occasionally snagged in a slight fight.
Pufferfish puffed, all full of glee,
Becoming pillows for sleepy free!

Seashells gossip as they sing,
Laughing at what sand crabs bring.
In this funny, foamy tide,
Every wave has joy inside!

Beneath the Surface

Bubbles laugh as fish swim by,
Turtles wear hats, oh me, oh my!
Clownfish tell their best dad jokes,
As seahorses twirl in playful pokes.

A hermit crab finds a new shell,
That used to house an old snail's swell.
Looks in the mirror, dares to pose,
With a jaunty wig of seaweed grows.

Eels in a band strum on the rocks,
Shaking their tails, they dance like flocks.
A chorus of clams claps in cheer,
As a mackerel winks—how queer!

Beneath the waves, nothing's as it seems,
Adventures explode in fishy dreams.
With laughter and silliness, we're set,
In a world of wonders, we won't forget!

Echoes of the Reef

In the reef, the chatter's grand,
Fish throwing parties, isn't it planned?
Coral polka dots and stripes,
Replace shy grins with funny wipes.

Mollusks wear a neat bow tie,
As sea otters learn how to fly.
Puffs of laughter through the blue,
Echo in tunes that feel brand new.

Blowfish boast their latest tricks,
While starfish join for quirky kicks.
With every splash, a giggle grows,
As seaweed twirls in rhythm flows.

Echoes bounce from rock to sand,
Every moment perfectly unplanned.
In this jolly ocean recess,
Life's a whimsy, nothing less!

Beneath the Shimmering Waves

Fish wear hats and dance all day,
While crabs hold parties, what do you say?
Seashells giggle, pearls throw cheer,
Underwater shenanigans, oh dear!

A lobster plays the ukulele nice,
With seaweed friends as their band of spice.
They serenade the octopus, quite bold,
With jokes and laughter, treasures unfold.

Turtles roll on tides of glee,
Dolphins prank with a splashy spree.
A starfish juggles, it's quite absurd,
In this wacky world, fun's assured!

So dive right in, the sea's a show,
Where laughter bubbles and good vibes flow.
In the depths below, there's always time,
For ocean frolic, and silly rhyme!

Brushstrokes of the Deep

A fish painted bright in polka dots,
Swims past a whale with a bucket of pots.
"Let's cook some soup!" the whale does say,
"Just make sure it's tasty and bright today!"

Sea cucumbers form a grand parade,
While sea anemones join the charade.
With brushes made of kelp, they start to paint,
Creating scenes that would make one faint!

A crab with glasses critiques the show,
"More bubbles, more sparkles!" Oh, how they glow!
The jellyfish glimmer while dancing their jig,
In this underwater art, all are a bigwig!

So when you think of the ocean's array,
Remember the laughter that colors the way.
With every stroke, a giggle, a jest,
In the gallery of waves, you'll find the best!

Whispers of the Salted Breeze

The gull cackles, sharing tales of the sea,
"Did you hear about the crab who danced with glee?"
A sea turtle chuckles, "Oh, what a sight!
He twirled in the waves, under the moonlight."

Barnacles gossip, they're quite the chat,
"Did you see that octopus in a top hat?"
He tipped his lid and spilled his ink,
Turning the ocean into a pink drink!

The waves join in, with a splash so loud,
As schools of fish gather, feeling proud.
A lobster chef sets the funniest meal,
Fried seaweed sandwiches, what a deal!

So let the salty breeze tease your hair,
With joyous stories filling the air.
Every wave whispers a giggle or two,
In this spirited world, dreams come true!

Currents of Imagination

A jellyfish floats, wearing a crown,
While fish in tuxedos swim up and down.
"Let's throw a ball!" the clownfish cried,
And with that, the ocean became a joyride!

Sea horses prance in their fancy attire,
While lobsters play charades, never tire.
"Guess what I am!" shouts the shrimp so spry,
With bubbles of laughter rising high!

With every direction, creativity swirls,
As seaweed dancers twirl and whirl.
The tides bring forth a splash of delight,
With friends all around, everything feels right!

So embrace the currents, let your mind soar,
In this playful sea, there's always more.
With a wink and a nudge, let laughter lead,
Through the flowing waters of daydreams freed!

Silence of the Blue

In the deep, where fish wear hats,
Octopus juggles with some squats.
Seahorses gossip, oh what a sight,
Nibbling their lunch and feeling quite light.

Clams play chess, oh what a bore,
While dolphins laugh and start a roar.
The sea lettuce waves, trying to dance,
But it trips on sand, oh what a chance!

Beyond the Moonscape

Starfish glide on invisible bikes,
Turtles race as if on hikes.
Shrimp throw parties, it's quite the scene,
While crabs play tunes on a tin can machine.

Jellyfish glow like disco balls,
Mermaids trade stories, and do water falls.
With laughter and bubbles, they fill the sea,
Who said the ocean can't be silly, you see?

Fragments of an Undersea Fantasy

Clownfish crack jokes, with a wink and a grin,
While eels hide away, they seldom join in.
The sea cucumbers prance with glee,
Declaring, "We're cooler than you'll ever be!"

Pufferfish puff in a boastful display,
"Look at us! We're scary, hooray!"
But one little tickle and who do we see?
A balloon that giggles, just as happy as can be.

Navigating Coral Currents

Nudibranchs in neon lead the parade,
While grumpy old grouper wants to invade.
"Hey, watch where you're going!" they yell with a cheer,
As a bubble floats by, adding to the beer!

Crabs with their claws dance a wobbly jig,
"Join us, you fools!" while they try to dig.
The laughter echoes, a bubbly delight,
Even the barnacles joined in the fight!

Secrets of the Coral Cathedral

In the depths where fish do prance,
Anemones swirl in a silly dance.
Starfish giggle, floating so high,
While sea cucumbers wave goodbye.

Clownfish wearing bright, funny hats,
Tell tales of octopuses and their chats.
Jellyfish bounce in their own way,
Turning the ocean blue into a play.

The seahorses twirl like they own the place,
Their fins flapping in such a strange grace.
A turtle snickers, lost in a loop,
As crabs join in, forming a troop.

And when the sun sets, colors alive,
The reef erupts, what a jolly dive!
Bubbles giggle, secrets to share,
In this cathedral, laughter fills the air.

Dance of the Marine Mirage

In waters where visions play hide and seek,
Waves softly ripple, tickling the cheek.
Dancing mermaids with laughter so loud,
Invite every fish to join their crowd.

Seahorses spinning in spirals so tight,
While squids jet off like a colorful kite.
Bubble-blowers make the sea foam delight,
As dolphins leap in a splashy height.

The otters slide on the slippery floor,
Paddling past critters who'd love to explore.
A lone angelfish, wearing a smile,
Sways to the currents with perfect style.

Under the moonlight, the laughter won't fade,
As all of the sea life joins the parade.
A festivity hidden, lost in the tides,
In this watery world, joy abides.

A Symphony of Shells

On a beach where the sun likes to play,
Shells gather 'round for a musical day.
A conch horn blows, calling friends to the scene,
While a sandpiper chirps, keeping time keen.

Clams tap their toes, just trying to keep,
While oysters grumble, but they're not too deep.
Tiny shrimps shuffle in a rhythmic line,
With laughter and tapping, oh how they shine!

A sea turtle hums a tune from the sea,
Each note echoing, wild and free.
While seagulls sing, perched high on their shelf,
Reminding us all, just be yourself.

With laughter and music, the shells all unite,
As the tide flows in, bringing new delight.
In this concert of life, we all join the swell,
Down by the shoreline, where secrets we tell.

The Silent Serenade

In the depths, where whispers twine,
Underwater critters begin to dine.
A snail plays slow, the conch hums a tune,
While fish throw a bash by the light of the moon.

Corals sway gently, feeling the groove,
Creating a rhythm that helps us move.
A pipefish winks, and the sea fans clap,
As all of the critters take a long nap.

Mantas drift in with grace and flair,
Their silent elegance fills up the air.
As sharks cast shadows, playful yet sly,
Scaring up giggles from shrimp passing by.

The quiet serenade spans far and wide,
As jellyfish shimmer in colors of pride.
In this underwater world, humor's concealed,
Where laughter abounds, and joy is revealed.

The Fishing Net's Song

In the ocean's dance, a fish forgot,
It wiggled and jiggled, stumbled a lot.
A fisherman laughed, with eyes like a child,
"You caught me!" said fish, with a grin so wild.

The net sang a tune, a snaggle-toothed rhyme,
As jellyfish jived in their gooey prime.
A crab started clapping with claws made of cheer,
And the seaweed swayed, like it had no fear.

Pulses of the Blue

There once was a tuna who dated a shark,
In a world of bubbles, they left quite a mark.
They'd swim in a loop, doing loop-dee-loops,
While clams all around formed a band of troops.

A dolphin dropped in with a wink and a flip,
"What's cooking, you two?" with a swirl and a dip.
"Just bass in our dreams, having fun in the tide,
With mermaids and sea cucumbers all by our side!"

Luminous Abyss

Deep in the depths, where the sunsets are green,
A glowworm whispered, "What do you mean?"
With a flick of its light, it turned quite mischief,
"I'm leading the fishes, like an underwater dish!"

An octopus giggled and danced in the dark,
With eight wheeled feet, it could surely leave a mark.
While anemones chuckled, with their tentacles swayed,
As they painted the night in a jellyfish parade.

Tidal Ballet

The waves took a bow, in a watery show,
With starfish applauding from their spots below.
A seal in a tux sang a high sea refrain,
While the sand crabs shuffled, in joy and in pain.

As currents waltzed in a frothy delight,
And the moon winked twice at the shimmering light.
The fish played the tambourine, quite out of sync,
In a tidal ballet that made dolphins blink.

Dance of the Aquatic Muses

In the depths, fish twirl and spin,
Bubbles burst with a cheeky grin.
Seaweed sways like a dancer's dress,
Octopuses giggle, oh what a mess!

Jellyfish hopping, a wobbly cheer,
Crabs for tap dance, oh dear, oh dear!
They shuffle and shuffle, oh what a sight,
Clownfish chuckle, it's pure delight!

Starfish flipping, they can't keep still,
Eels attempt cartwheels, what a thrill!
A turtle giggles, takes a leap,
Splashing water, the ocean's sweet peep!

This underwater rave, so full of cheer,
With creatures jiving, spreading the jeer.
In the depths, both silly and spry,
Join the dance, just give it a try!

Reefside Reverberations

A parrotfish sings, with scales so bright,
Bubbles of laughter in the warm sunlight.
A clownfish tries to tell a joke,
But all the sea cucumbers just choke!

Sea turtles groan as they twist and glide,
While shrimps in a conga line take pride.
A starfish shimmies, but oh what a flop,
The ocean's laughing, it just won't stop!

Coral fans waving, they join in the fun,
With sea urchins bouncing under the sun.
A dolphin calls out, "Let's have a ball!"
The whole reef joins in, answering the call!

As waves whisper tales from the ocean's deep,
Creatures gather, their friendship they'll keep.
With giggles and gurgles, they fill the sea,
A ripple of joy, wild and free!

Underwater Serenade

In the silence where fish skitter and play,
A sea anemone hums all day.
Sponges bouncing to a rhythm unknown,
With giggling shrimp making it their own!

The manta rays glide, with grace and a twist,
In a limbo contest, none shall be missed.
A sardine choir singing flatly in tune,
While a crab mimes under the bright blue moon!

A seahorse trots like it's in a parade,
Synchronized swimming, not one bit delayed.
Clams start to clap, oh what a racket,
A bubble blubber joins in the bracket!

Each coral branch sways, laughing in glee,
As fish pass the beat, like leaves from a tree.
In this watery world, oh delightfully grand,
An orchestra playing, by nature's own hand!

Celestial Waters

Splashing stars twinkle in fluid embrace,
A fishy fairy dance, oh what a space!
Pufferfish puff, trying to impress,
But blowfish squeak, making a mess!

Bubble-blowing dolphins, tones of glee,
Sardines spinning like a disco spree.
An octopus juggling, with eight arms spread,
While seahorses wonder what's in their head!

With kelp in their hair, the sea urchins pout,
"What's this commotion? What's it about?"
They wriggle and bob, just want to partake,
In the joyous festivities, for laughter's sake!

From below the waves, a magical show,
The aquatic jesters put on the flow.
In waters celestial, laughter runs deep,
The ocean smiles wide, it's a dream full of peep!

Melodies from the Reef

Bubbles rise, fish do a jig,
A crab in a top hat, doing a gig.
Starfish claps with a happy cheer,
As the seaweed sways, oh so dear.

Turtles sing in falsetto delight,
While shrimps prepare for a dance-off tonight.
They twirl and they spin with silly glee,
In this underwater jubilee!

A clam's got rhythm, it opens wide,
The dolphins jump, oh, what a ride!
With every flip, there's laughter and fun,
Who knew the sea could be number one?

So come join the party where shells do chime,
In a splashing good time that'll last for all time!
With oceanic tunes that tickle your feet,
These melodies from the reef can't be beat.

The Dance of Tide Pools

In a tide pool party, the seaweed sways,
Anemones bop in the sunlight's rays.
Shrimps wear bowties, all dressed up neat,
Crabs do the shimmy with comic defeat.

Periwinkle snails glide in a race,
While sea stars practice their best ballet grace.
"Watch me spin!" says a plucky little fish,
In this watery world, there's always a wish.

A plump sea cucumber joins in the fun,
Saying, "Why not? I've only just begun!"
A clam shimmies, shells click-tap,
All join together for a tide pool clap.

As waves dance by, they can't help but cheer,
For underwater antics bring cheer far and near.
So dive right in, let your worries erase,
In the dance of tide pools, it's the silliest place!

Synchronized Splendor

In the bubble parade, seahorses align,
Flipping and flopping, it's simply divine.
With synchronized moves, they twirl and glide,
As octopuses giggle, they loom and hide.

The fish form a conga, scales shine so bright,
With a sparkle they shimmer, a fabulous sight.
A lionfish leads with a wave of its fin,
While clumsy doodlebugs attempt to join in.

"Don't lose the beat!" shouts a lobster with flair,
As sea cucumbers shuffle without any care.
In this ocean cabaret, it's truly a blast,
Watching critters collaborate, laughter amassed.

So rally the waves and bring in the crowd,
For synchronized splendor, let's laugh out loud!
In this splashy performance, take front row seats,
Every fin, every tail, brings infectious beats!

Lullabies of the Liquid Realm

As the moonlight glimmers on waters so deep,
Little fish gather, they're ready to leap.
A gentle tide whispers with soft, dreamy sighs,
Under big, grinning whales with twinkling eyes.

Seahorses nap on soft coral beds,
While jellyfish sway in their slumber thread.
With sea turtles crooning in sweet harmony,
Lullabies rock the currents, wild and free.

Starfish hum tunes like they're in a band,
Bubbles drift softly, hand in hand.
The ocean's embrace, a blanket so warm,
In this liquid realm, laughter is the norm.

So close your eyes, let the water cradle,
In this merry dream, laughter will ladle.
With cuddly creatures creating a theme,
It's all peaceful bliss, in a heavenly dream.

Drama of the Deep Blue

A fish donned a top hat, quite proud of his flair,
He danced with a crab who lost one of his legs.
They twirled through a garden of seaweed and snare,
Bubbles popping like popcorn – how they laughed 'til they begged.

A turtle in glasses worked hard on a play,
He wrote of a dolphin who dreamed she could fly.
The jellyfish juiced it, a script on display,
While seahorses critiqued and the clownfish said 'Why?'

An octopus juggled with shells and a shoe,
His eight arms in motion a marvelous sight!
The audience gasped, "What will he do?"
As an eel dressed as Elvis made the act light.

Then came the grand finale, the crowd burst with glee,
When a whale serenaded, "Just call me a star!"
They threw sea cucumbers, what a raucous spree,
In the deep blue, the laughter rolled near and far!

Weaving Through Currents

The jelly pals were sewing a bubble skirt,
Stitching with giggles and threads made of light.
They asked a shy clam, 'Do you want to flirt?'
He opened his shell, and oh what a fright!

A squirrelfish fought hard to join in the fun,
But tangled in bubbles, he churned like a twirler.
The seahorse tucked in for a ride, then they run,
The laughter erupted; they glided, a whirl-er.

A starfish in shades was the coolest of all,
With snappy comebacks and moves full of charm.
He pranced through the reef with a shimmy and crawl,
And warned a poor puffer not to raise alarm.

They twirled through the tides, quite the viral craze,
With currents that tickled and flowed like a stream.
Each splash made them giggle, lost in their ways,
In the warm ocean's quilt, they were living a dream.

Through the Glistening Waters

A crab in sunglasses strutted along,
He invented a dance that confused all the fish.
The clownfish joined in with a bubble-blown song,
They giggled and flipped, made a mess of the dish.

A dolphin appeared with a splash of delight,
She juggled some shells while riders did cheer.
But a passing old grouper just grumbled, 'Not right!'
The mollusks all snorted; they knew it was clear.

The sea turtles joined in, all geared up for fun,
With snorkels and flippers and snacks from the reef.
They surfed on the waves till the setting of sun,
Creating a ruckus, new tales to belief.

The waters sparkled with laughter and glee,
As fish broke into the most wobbly dance.
Tides turned to music, wild and carefree,
With each flip and splash came a marvelous chance.

The Underwater Kaleidoscope

The angelfish twirled in a costume of light,
While starfish played catch with a jellyfish foe.
A shrimp in a bowtie asserted, 'I'm right!'
As bubbles erupted, the humor would flow.

A flounder spoke wisdom, or so he believed,
But a parrotfish chuckled, 'Oh, what a jest!'
With comments so silly, the crowd was deceived,
And they rolled on the sand where the creatures now rest.

A sea cucumber whispered a joke to a crab,
'The ocean is deep, but my humor runs wide!'
They share nearly everything, even their drab,
Yet laughing together, they sought to confide.

Then came the big show, a spectacle bright,
As mermaids with harps serenaded the throng.
From the depths of the blue, oh what a delight,
In this kaleidoscope, every laugh felt like song!

Colors Beneath the Surface

In a world of fish with silly grins,
Bubbles dance like they're doing spins.
Starfish wear hats, oh what a sight,
Clownfish joke under the soft moonlight.

Jellyfish float with a wobbly sway,
Sardines gather for a cabaret play.
Corals giggle in hues of pink,
Seahorses poke with a wink, wink, wink.

The octopus juggles his dinner plate,
While turtles debate which shell is great.
A crab does a jig to a catchy tune,
As dolphins dance 'neath the laughing moon.

And in this world, laughter's the key,
With fishy puns that are fresh and free.
Under the waves where the fun resides,
The ocean's laughter forever abides.

Fantasia in Fins

Fins flap like flags in a fishy parade,
Whales wear bow ties, they've got it made.
Tropical fish paint the sea in glee,
They throw a bash, just wait and see!

Clownfish tell jokes, how they do tease,
"Why don't we ever get lost at sea?"
Turtles skate on algae like magic glue,
While shrimp do the conga and cha-cha too.

The seahorses prance with elegant flair,
In their little tuxedos, beyond compare.
Anemones laugh, they twist and twine,
In this underwater cabaret divine.

And so they swim, in a splashy trance,
Where bubbles and giggles join in the dance.
Under the waves, let the fun commence,
With fins of delight and a dash of suspense.

Woven in Seafoam

Kelp forests sway like a bohemian hat,
Where starfish gossip and lobsters chat.
A mermaid sips tea with a wink of her eye,
While crabs in tuxedos sip punch on the fly.

Seafoam whirls in a frothy embrace,
Fish sport top hats for a grand showcase.
An octopus tries to braid a sweet strand,
While sea turtles snap selfies—oh, how they'll stand!

The clownfish giggle as they zoom and glide,
Spreading joy like confetti, a vibrant tide.
Seashells chime in with their bubbly cheer,
Echoing laughter from far and near.

Down in the depths, where silliness rules,
Creatures unite, like whimsical fools.
Woven in laughter, a tapestry bright,
In the ocean's embrace, everything feels right.

The Ocean's Palette

With brushes made from seaweed and sand,
The fish paint their faces—oh, isn't it grand?
Colors splash wildly, let the brush fly,
In this underwater art show, oh my!

The eels encircle with sparkly flair,
While squids throw ink like magic in air.
Angelfish prance in a dazzling display,
As clams crack jokes, making waves in the bay.

Each splash is a giggle, each stroke a cheer,
Creating reminders that fun's always near.
The sea's an artist, with humor its brush,
In a whimsical world, there's never a hush.

So dive in with laughter, let the fun soar,
In this ocean of wonders, there's always much more.
The palette of laughter, bright colors collide,
In the swirl of the sea, where delight can't hide.

The Aquatic Tapestry

A fish in a bowtie, what a sight,
Dancing with bubbles, oh what a delight.
The octopus juggling, with style galore,
Inviting a clam, who just wants to snore.

Starfish singing in harmony bright,
While turtles are playing their favorite fight.
A seaweed waltz, in a sparkling trance,
Everyone joins in, they just love to dance.

Anemone tickles a crab in a hat,
That mischievous snapper, what's with the spat?
Jellyfish laughing, in a swirling parade,
While dolphins play games of light-hearted charade.

Sardines in sequins, all glimmer and gleam,
Making grand entrances, just like a dream.
This oceanic tale, with humor to share,
In a realm of the quirky, no one has a care.

Mysteries in Molten Color

A seahorse sipping on bubble tea,
Confused as a clownfish in a jamboree.
The barnacles gossip, with shells all aglow,
While the flounder floats like a showbiz pro.

Neon corals wear funny hats,
As the angelfish gossip about where they're at.
A pufferfish laughs with a cheeky grin,
Telling tall tales of the great shark within.

Scuba divers waving, oh what a sight,
In costumes so wild, they startle the night.
An eel on a skateboard, catching some rays,
Surfing the currents in wacky ways.

Starry-eyed fishes giggle and play,
In a kaleidoscope world, they frolic away.
With colors so vivid, smiles so bright,
This underwater circus brings pure delight.

Fantastical Flotsam

A mermaid who sings with a cat on her knee,
Teaching the dolphins to climb up a tree.
The jellybeans swimming, all rainbow and swirled,
Telling their secrets in a sugary world.

Bubbles do cartwheels in giggling clusters,
While shrimp in tuxedos throw fanciful flusters.
The trout in a top hat makes quite the toast,
To the whale who juggles—a delightful host.

Crabs in the corner play poker for fun,
Betting their shells in the warm, shiny sun.
With a wink and a nudge, they dash and they spin,
Shuffling and grinning, it's a game they all win.

A tidal wave giggles as it rolls on the sand,
Tickling the toes of an unsuspecting band.
With laughter and splashes, this whimsic sea stream,
Creates quite the ruckus in a dream of a dream.

Beneath the Sunlit Waters

In a bowl of clear jelly, the fish tell a tale,
Of a crab in a vest who's completely turned pale.
A dolphin on roller skates zooms in for a show,
Wheeling around jellyfish, putting on a glow.

Turtles with sunglasses, lounging with flair,
Sipping on seaweed, they haven't a care.
The clams tap their feet to a bubbly refrain,
While the shrimp throw confetti, as wild as a train.

A seahorse surfing a wave made of foam,
Can't quite decide if he's far from his home.
With seagrass confetti floating down from above,
This show under waves is a dance full of love.

With laughter and giggles, the ocean unfolds,
Each fin and each scale shares its stories untold.
In this vibrant world, where joy is the key,
Beneath the bright surface, it's all wackily free.

Dreams on the Ocean Floor

Bubbles rise, fish wiggle with glee,
A squid plays the sax, just wait and see.
The starfish dance on their bumpy backs,
While crabs in bow ties plot secret attacks.

A dolphin sneezes, the sea laughs aloud,
Mermaids giggle, just too proud.
With seaweed wigs and jellyfish hats,
The gossip flows, oh, the chit-chats!

An octopus juggles, what a sight,
As turtles race, taking flight.
Seahorses laugh at the shrimp's big dreams,
In this underwater world of silly schemes.

So take a dive into the blue,
Where whimsy abounds and joy renews.
In the depths, with laughter galore,
The ocean floor is never a bore.

The Vibrant Underbelly

In the deep, the colors explode,
Anemones dance in a vibrant code.
A clownfish laughs, painting a smile,
While lobsters waltz in a jazzy style.

Shrimp throw parties, with disco lights,
While eels pull pranks, giving silly frights.
The parrotfish chatter, oh what a fuss,
As sardines swarm in a glittery bus!

A flounder plays hide-and-seek with grace,
The sea cucumbers join the race.
With each wiggly tail and every splash,
Laughter resounds, oh what a bash!

So come take a dip in this lively scene,
Where every fin dances, bright and keen.
In the vibrant depths, feel the joy swell,
Underbelly magic, casting a spell!

Visions from the Brine

From the briny depths, a giggle erupts,
As a fish in a bowler hat suddenly jumps.
Seahorses whisper secrets so grand,
While squid serve tea with a delicate hand.

An otter slips on a slick seaweed floor,
And seals wear glasses, just begging for more.
The jellyfish glow with radiant flair,
While crabs tell tales with a sassy air.

A fish with a mustache struts through the scene,
Playing the lute, so cool and serene.
Octopuses wink with eight lined-up quirks,
Creating a ruckus with all their neat works.

So let's dive deep into visions abound,
Where laughter and bubbles are found all around.
In the brine, the fun never glimmers away,
It's a wacky world where the weirdos play!

Shells and Stardust

On sandy floors, where shells shimmer bright,
Starfish wearing sunglasses bask in the light.
Crabs don their hats, the tailors of fate,
Creating beachwear that's truly first-rate.

With seashells and stardust, they throw a parade,
Mermaids conduct with a bubbly charade.
The clams push the conch to get the beat right,
While barnacles join the dance with delight.

A clam taps its foot to the ocean's big band,
Turtles cheer on, driving all the land.
The water twirls as the bubbles burst free,
With each wavy line, hilarity we see!

So gather your shells, let's join this great show,
Where the ocean's the stage and fun's set to flow.
Under the waves, with laughter and cheer,
Shells and stardust, the best time of year!

Reflections of the Abyss

A fish in a tux, quite dapper,
Swims past a clam, who's a scrapper.
With pearls as her bling, she's a sight,
She flips her lid, what a delight!

Deep down, the octopus prances,
In eight different shoes, doing glances.
He twirls and he whirls, such a blast,
Making jellyfish giggle at last!

A turtle with shades and a grin,
Zooms by a snail, who's slow to begin.
"Catch me if you can!" he yells with glee,
While the snail just sighs, "Oh, woe is me!"

A seahorse joins the dance, so spry,
In a polka-dot suit, oh my oh my!
He whips his tail, and the waves align,
As the whole deep sea joins in the line!

The Rainbow's Underbelly

A crab with a cap and a giant loud horn,
Plays tunes that echo from dusk until morn.
The fish gather round for a splashy parade,
Dancing in bubbles, they're not even afraid!

Starfish in slippers do goofy ballet,
While whales in a chorus sing night into day.
"Fins up!" they shout in a joyful delight,
As a dolphin somersaults into the night!

Pufferfish posing with style that's so smart,
Inflates with each joke, oh, what a fine art!
Their laughs make the seaweed do jiggle and sway,
While plankton join in for a swell cabaret!

As squids do their best to juggle some shells,
Anemones chuckle, they know all too well.
With laughter aplenty that bubbles and gleams,
Underwater raves become silly sweet dreams!

In the Shadow of Sea Fountains

Bubbles are popping like corn in a pot,
A mermaid's lost comb, she's searching a lot.
Fish tell tall tales of things they have seen,
While a crab criticizes, "That's just too mean!"

An electric eel throws a wild disco,
Flashing bright lights, putting on quite a show.
Clownfish in costumes, all mismatched and bright,
They're searching for snacks but can't take a bite!

Seagulls sit high, dropping fries from the sky,
While sea turtles ponder, "Why, oh why?"
The seahorses giggle, taking notes for their class,
On how to float gracefully and keep up with the mass.

With laughter resounding in currents and swirls,
The sea sings a song where the oddest joy twirls.
Everyone dances beneath the sea's fountains,
In the underwater chaos, fun joy surmounts!

The Heartbeat of the Ocean

A clam with a crown sits pretty and proud,
While oysters collaborate, creating a crowd.
They throw a pearl party with gusto and flair,
As the jellyfish float, waving without a care!

Fish quiz the sea cucumbers, "What's your trick?"
To stay very still, without mingling, quick!
But a grouper shouts loudly, "You've got to be brave!
Join in all the laughter, don't just be a wave!"

The angler fish grins with a light on his head,
Charming small fish while they flee in a spread.
"Wait! I was joking," he yells in dismay,
But the fish just roll off, "That's not how we play!"

All together they frolic, with bubbles they gleam,
In the currents of joy, life's one big fun dream.
In this wild ocean, with smiles on the face,
Each heartbeat's a giggle, a quirky embrace!

Colors of the Abyss

In a sea of shades, I find my groove,
Fish wear hats and dance, what a move!
Purple polka dots swim with flair,
While jellyfish juggle without a care.

Giant clams play chess, it's quite the sight,
They call the moves with a clammy delight.
Bubbles giggle and tickle your toes,
As seaweed whistles and hilarity grows.

Starfish on stilts prance in the sand,
Waving their arms like a rock band.
An octopus juggles five little stars,
While dolphins zoom by in their fancy cars.

Oh, the colors swirl in underwater fun,
Where every laugh bubbles up like the sun.
Under the waves, let your worries cease,
Dive into joy; it's a slippery peace.

Fluid Fantasies

Mermaids trade tales, sipping sea foam,
In fishy cafes, they all call home.
One has a cat that swims like a pro,
While crabs play the piano, putting on a show.

Turtles wear shades, lounging in style,
Laughing at currents, they swim with a smile.
A whale sings pop, oh what a thrill,
Bubbles bounce back, they dance at will.

Seahorses gossip, swirling about,
With tales of the shipwreck and the odd shout.
Anemones bloom, pink and blue,
As seagulls dive down for a laugh or two.

In this fluid realm where oddities reign,
Fun swims around in this watery lane.
Join the madcap with fins, take a leap,
Dream of the depths, where silliness sleeps.

Secrets of the Sea

What do the waves whisper under the moon?
The sea's got jokes, like a clown's balloon.
Crabs wear mustaches, looking quite dapper,
And sea cucumbers act as a trapper.

Fish hold a meeting, discussing their puns,
Who's the best swimmer? Oh, the fun runs!
A porcupine fish rolls in laughter,
As octopuses plot their lobster disaster.

A treasure chest bursts with glittery cheer,
With candy and trinkets, it's hard to steer.
Every merchant fish has a story to share,
Conch shells gossip; who needs a fair?

So while the tide sings its watery song,
The secrets of sea life keep laughter strong.
Dive deep for the humor and joy it weaves,
In ocean's embrace, where the whimsy believes.

The Coral's Embrace

In the reef's warm hug, laughter's a blast,
Sardines form lines, dancing so fast.
Colorful critters play peek-a-boo,
While clownfish giggle, all painted in hue.

The coral winks at the passing fish,
"Join me for lunch? What's your favorite dish?"
Anemones cheer as they sway side to side,
Underwater parties are quite the ride.

Guppies and gobies slap high-fives with flair,
As they spin and swirl without a care.
Eels tell tall tales and tickle each fin,
In this goofy kingdom, let the fun begin!

The coral puts on a dazzling show,
Where laughter blooms and the giggles grow.
In the ocean's heart, have faith, and believe,
You might just find magic in the sea's weave.

Chasing Ocean Light

In a game of hide and seek,
The fish wear masks and sneak.
They wiggle, they dance, full of glee,
As I trip on seaweed, oh me!

A crab in a top hat gives a wink,
He offers me soda, then a drink.
With bubbles rising, laughter flows,
As squids juggle shells in a show!

Jellyfish sway like party hats,
Bouncing to tunes played by seashell chats.
I slip on a clam, what a delightful mess,
The ocean's jokes, I must confess!

As sunlight sparkles on the waves,
I join the dance, the ocean saves.
With dolphins laughing in their spree,
This underwater life is pure glee!

Aquatic Echoes

The seahorses line up for a race,
With tiny helmets, they speed and chase.
An octopus calls it a relay run,
But slips on seaweed—oh, what fun!

A starfish spins like a disco ball,
While clownfish giggle, having a ball.
The sea cucumbers join in the beat,
Tapping their tentacles, such a treat!

Bubbles rise like a soda pop fizz,
As tides tickle shores, feel the whizz.
A whale sings songs that are quite absurd,
While the shrimp share jokes—oh, how they stirred!

In this watery world, all things align,
Where laughter and splashes truly entwine.
With a wink from a turtle, life seems to zoom,
In the kingdom of waves, there's always room!

Where Sea Meets Sky

At sunrise, crabs toast with a cheer,
While gulls fly around in a dizzying sphere.
A splash from a dolphin, what a surprise,
With a twist and a leap, he's off to the skies!

A clam holds a party, with lanterns aglow,
As fish wear their best, for the show of the show.
The anemones sway to the jolly tunes,
While sea turtles dance, beneath bright moons.

The sun dips low, casting shadows and light,
In this wavy world, oh, everything's bright!
A manta ray twirls, in a pirouette swirl,
As sea stars giggle, what a joyful whirl!

And when night falls, with stars all around,
There's laughter and tales that know no bound.
With splashy jokes in the soothing tide's call,
Where sea meets sky, there's magic for all!

Harmonics of the Current

In the current where the laughter flows,
A fish chorus sings, in colorful prose.
With bubble bursts like giggles that rise,
They jest and jest, under the bright skies.

An eel tells stories with a wiggly twist,
While clams turn red, lost in the mist.
With seaweed swaying, they dance like a troupe,
While the waves thump a splendid loop!

Anemones blush, oh what a sight,
As they shimmy and shake, full of delight.
A hermit crab joins in, wearing a sock,
While the fish all laugh, oh what a shock!

Beneath the moonlight, jokes still resound,
In this splashy choir, joy knows no bound.
With every ripple, life plays its part,
In the harmonics of this oceanic art!

Underwater Reverie

Bubbles rise with tales untold,
Fish with hats, the brave and bold.
Seaweed dances, waving high,
Octopus painting the evening sky.

Jellyfish bounce like they're on air,
Clownfish giggle without a care.
Turtles comically stuck in time,
Sing a tune with a silly rhyme.

Crabs hold parties on the sand,
Spinning tales of a treasure grand.
While starfish cheer with a little glee,
As sea cucumbers boogie with me.

In this world of splashes and frights,
Everything glimmers under starry nights.
Forget the worries above the foam,
In the deep blue, we find our home.

Tides of Whimsy

Surfers fish with their nets of dreams,
Playful shells jingle, or so it seems.
Waves tickle toes with laughter so bright,
Seahorses racing, what a sight!

Squids in glasses, looking so chic,
All the fish gather for a sneak peek.
Crabs with swagger, snap and clap,
Join the party; don't miss the map!

Starfish juggling in a funky way,
Dolphins dance, splashing all day.
Mollusks grooving, their shells aflare,
In the whirlpool of joy, we share.

Sharks tell jokes, who would've thought?
Even the deep has laughter caught.
The tide rolls on with a wink and a nudge,
Join the mirth, there's nothing to judge.

The Reef's Lullaby

In a patch of warmth, a turtle snores,
Fish brush past with gossip galore.
Corals hum a soothing tune,
While minnows shimmy under the moon.

Anemones play hide and seek,
Starfish giggles keep the reef unique.
Lobsters tap dance in their own parades,
All wearing hats, in the ocean shades.

An octopus croons a wacky ballad,
Whales serenade with a funny salad.
Clownfish jesters prance about,
Chasing their tails, filled with doubt.

The seabed shakes with laughter below,
As funny fish put on a show.
In this underwater serenade,
Every dream and giggle cascade.

Echoes of the Abyss

Beneath the waves, where oddities play,
Fish in tuxedos, what a display!
Giant sea urchins throw a bash,
In a bubbly world, there's nothing brash.

Crashing currents sing sweet tunes,
Tangled kelp sways to joyful moons.
Grouper groan in comedic style,
While feather stars twirl with a smile.

Whales' belly laughs resonate wide,
Come join the circus, let's take a ride.
Pufferfish frolic with zest and grace,
In this deep bluesy, giggle-filled space.

From depths where silliness reigns supreme,
Echoes of fun, a sparkling dream.
So dive in deep, leave worries behind,
In this ocean wonder, joy you will find.

The Music of Ocean Dreams

Underwater sounds make me grin,
A fishy band begins to spin.
Seaweed dances, it's quite a scene,
With crustaceans playing tambourine.

A clam so wise gives quite a show,
While flipping flippers, a dolphin's glow.
They gather shells to form a bridge,
And sing silly tunes, with no fridge!

The octopus has lost its hat,
As jellyfish join with a splat!
The crabs tap dance on the sand,
Bravo ocean! A strange band!

Sea cucumbers sway with a shock,
Wiggling grooves around the rock.
The pufferfish inflates with pride,
Underwater fun we can't decide!

Shifting Sands and Sea Stars

On a beach where laughter sings,
The sea stars sip on fizzy things.
They squint and giggle, what a sight,
As sands shift under the moonlight.

A crab in shades, looking divine,
Claims he's the king of the shoreline.
With a flip and flap, he stakes his claim,
While seagulls shout, they know his name!

The sandcastles wave flags so bright,
Shifting shapes, there's a silly fight.
Seashells cheer from their sandy seat,
As waves crash in with a tickle feat!

Dolphins race with a splashy cheer,
Each one thinks they're a new frontier.
With giggling waves that poke the shore,
The sea's a jester, always wanting more!

Revealing the Unknown Depths

Bubbles rise from the depths unseen,
A mermaid holds a magazine.
She winks at eels, who try to pose,
While snails gossip in brightly colored clothes.

A treasure chest full of silly hats,
Fish dressed up as acrobats.
They twirl and twist, such a delight,
In ocean's theater, all dressed so bright!

An urchin wants to be a star,
With sequins shining from afar.
He steals the show with a funny dance,
Not shy at all, he takes his chance!

The depths unfold with giggling glee,
A clownfish dons a wig like me.
With laughter echoing in the blue,
The underwater world's a quirky zoo!

Underwater Echoes

Splashing around, the sea cucumbers play,
While seahorses trot in a glamorous way.
Echoes of laughter ripple so bright,
As fish join in under the moonlight.

The good old coral bands that can sing,
Make seaweed swing like a funny fling.
A grouper jokes in a ruffled tale,
While schools of fish set up a sail.

Bubble-blowing turtles compete with a grin,
Each puff of air is a bubbly win.
Sardines twist in a synchronized spree,
They giggle and giggle, it's pure jubilee!

With every ripple, a story unfolds,
As starfish spin yarns of shimmering gold.
In echoes of water, we find our cheer,
A funny swim in an ocean so dear!

Whirl of Marine Colors

A fish in a tutu does the cha-cha,
With bubbles popping like a soda!
Octopus juggling with eight busy arms,
While a shrimp taps to the underwater charms.

Starfish playing cards, what a sight!
Cowabunga clams dance through the night.
A sea horse wearing a tiny top hat,
Sipping plankton tea while chatting with a bat.

Purple seaweed twirls like a scenic vine,
As whales sing tunes, oh so divine!
The ocean's a carnival, bright and spry,
Where fish wear sunglasses, oh my, oh my!

A kraken with a flair for dramatic poses,
Sprinkles confetti from its leafy roses.
The ocean floor's alive with playful screams,
In this wacky world of finned daydreams.

Beneath Moonlit Waves

Under the moon, a lobster does the can-can,
While jellyfish float like soft, glowing fans.
Turtles play paddy-cake, how absurd,
As dolphins join in with a splash and a bird!

Squid having tea parties, fancy and bright,
Sipping on seaweed till the morning light.
A clam cracks jokes that make everyone giggle,
While starfish wiggle, dance, and wiggle!

A mermaid juggles pearls under the stars,
As sea anemones wear matching guitars.
The sardines form a conga line so fine,
Wiggling through waters like they're on cloud nine!

Beneath the glow, the laughter swells,
In a world where fun is cast in shells.
With waves as the background and fish as the band,
Let's dance till morning in this magical land!

Dreams of an Aquatic Muse

In waters blue, a goldfish dreams,
Of swimming in shoals of jelly-bean creams.
A crab in a bowtie mixes drinks,
While sea cucumbers talk, and giggle, and wink!

The anemones gossip, their colors ablaze,
Sharing wild tales from their underwater phase.
Clownfish wearing clown wigs with flair,
Host a comedy night in their cozy lair!

Sharks in tuxedos discuss the next meal,
Snickering wildly, oh, what a deal!
Seahorses playing poker, bluffing for fun,
As the sun dips low, the party's begun!

With laughter and bubbles, the ocean sings,
In a wacky world of fins and wings.
Where sea light twinkles with mischievous hues,
We dance in our dreams, beneath watery blues.

Pulse of the Ocean Floor

Down below, the party's in full swing,
With sand dollars twirling, they're wearing bling!
An octopus chef prepares a grand feast,
As fish come running, the fun will not cease.

Starry-eyed squids put on a light show,
While shrimp wear capes, ready to go!
Blowfish pumping up with pride,
As seahorses boogie, showing their glide!

Clams play instruments made from old shells,
While sea turtles hum out the ocean's swells.
Bubbles rise high, popping with cheer,
In the pulse of the ocean, no room for fear!

A fish in a bow decides to break dance,
As rays snicker softly, caught in a trance.
From the ocean floor to the sunlit waves,
Life's a funny frolic in this world it paves!

Mysteries in the Blues

In a garden where fish like to play,
Tropical colors brighten the day.
A lobster dances with a jellyfish,
Making odd requests, what a silly wish!

A dolphin sings in a goofy way,
Turning seaweed into a bouquet.
The octopus wears a top hat so proud,
While clams clap shells, they laugh out loud.

A sea turtle rolls, quite a sight,
Wobbling like it's had too much light.
Crabs throw a party with shells for chairs,
While starfish gossip, exchanging smears.

Bubbles are giggles, laughter flows,
As seahorses twirl, they put on shows.
Each wave holds secrets, wild and strange,
In this underwater world full of change.

Luminescent Horizons

Where the sun dips low beneath the tide,
Creatures glimmer where secrets abide.
A pufferfish tries on a fancy coat,
While a clownfish juggles, giving a quote.

Beneath the stars, a crab takes the stage,
Aerial antics—what a hilarious page!
Seagulls are hecklers, throwing their chips,
While the sea urchin is pulling some flips.

Octopuses tickle, what a strange sport,
With ink clouds raised, it's a swirling court.
A shrimp with shades struts down the street,
While snails race by on their slow-motion feet.

Under the cloak of the deep, silly dreams,
Where laughter bubbles up in funny streams.
Every wave a chuckle, every splash a grin,
Join this odd crew where the fun begins.

Undersea Dreams

In the depths where the sillies collide,
Fish play poker in a clamshell wide.
A whale belly laughs, it's a real good time,
While plankton sing out their nursery rhyme.

A starfish paints with hues so bright,
Creating portraits that tickle delight.
Eels do a dance, all wiggly and slick,
While sea cucumbers pull off a trick.

A crab uses its claw as a brush,
Crafting doodles with a big, silly fuss.
Anemones giggle, waving their arms,
Luring in fish with their flowery charms.

Serpentine currents, they swirl and spin,
A mermaid chuckles, her laughter a win.
In this world where the whimsy takes flight,
The sea becomes laughter, day turns to night.

Ephemeral Beauty Beneath

In the glimmering depths where the giggles reside,
Fish wear tuxedos, a formal tide.
A sea cucumber dreams of a night on the town,
While jellyfish float in their gowns of renown.

The seahorse sways, a most dapper gent,
With a mustache made of seaweed and scent.
Crabs gossip loudly about ocean pride,
As they shuffle along on their sideways slide.

A parrotfish shouts, "I'm the best of the best!"
Competing with clowns in marine humor fest.
While barnacles peek from their spots on the rock,
Counting the laughs, like ticks on a clock.

With laughter echoing in the cool ocean bliss,
The quirkiness blooms, and you can't help but miss.
Every moment's a jest, in this watery land,
Where finned friends gather, so merry and grand.

Dreamscapes of the Deep

Bubbles float like tiny hopes,
A dolphin wearing funny clothes,
They giggle as they splash around,
Making friends with fish who clown.

Octopus in a chef's hat,
Stirring soup with a long spatula,
A sea turtle joins the feast,
Balancing a plate of seaweed cheese.

Seahorses dance in polka dots,
Throwing parties in their spots,
With jellyfish as disco balls,
They boogie till the ocean calls.

Mermaids singing silly rhymes,
Tickling crabs in flowing lines,
Each wave brings a laughing tune,
Where the sea meets the bright blue moon.

A Canvas of Waves

The painter's brush—a whale's tail dive,
Colors swirling like a jive,
Starfish hold their own art show,
With jellybeans strewn below.

A clownfish in a tutu spins,
Showing off his wiggly fins,
While sea cucumbers drum away,
Making beats throughout the day.

In the reef, the snails parade,
With tiny hats they've carefully made,
Crabs don shades to look so slick,
Creating waves with every flick.

The ocean floor is quite the sight,
With playful creatures taking flight,
Each wave a brush stroke in delight,
Painting laughter, day and night.

Song of the Seafoam

The seafoam sings a bubbly song,
Inviting all to come along,
Seashells clapping, crabs keep time,
In a rhythm silly and sublime.

Starfish jam on sandy shores,
While otters tap on ocean floors,
A riptide mimics a party's flow,
Going round and round—let's go, let's go!

Little fishes wear their best suits,
Marching in their shiny boots,
With every splash, their laughter grows,
As the tide tickles their toes.

Eels twist like dancers on parade,
In a lively, aquatic charade,
As the sun dips low, a golden beam,
We celebrate this frothy dream!

Odes to the Ocean Floor

Anemones sway like they're in a trance,
Pantomiming their silly dance,
With starry skies above, so blue,
They giggle at the view anew.

The clam debates with a wise old fish,
Whispering secrets, making a wish,
While sea sponges crack the jokes,
Sending shivers in laughing pokes.

The floor is littered with bright, odd things,
From pirates' gold to mermish rings,
Each treasure has a story told,
In the wavy depths, brave and bold.

In this underwater world of cheer,
Fun surprises lurking near,
With laughter echoing near and far,
As the light dances on each bizarre.

www.ingramcontent.com/pod-product-compliance
Lightning Source LLC
Chambersburg PA
CBHW060117230426
43661CB00003B/226